Registry of Guitar Tutors

GUITAR LESSONS

ROCK AND METAL

BY TONY SKINNER & ANDY DRUDY

A CIP record for this publication is available from the British Library.
ISBN: 1-898466-77-7

© 2005 Registry Publications Ltd

Lessons written by Tony Skinner; edited by Laurence Harwood.
Music composed by Tony Skinner; performed by Andy Drudy.
Music and text typesetting by Laurence Harwood.

Published by

Registry Mews, 11-13 Wilton Rd, Bexhill, E. Sussex, TN40 1HY

Printed and bound in Great Britain

CONTENTS

Introduction   4

Notation Guide   5

Lesson 1 – Power Chords [CD track 2 - 9]   7

Lesson 2 – Classic Rock Riffing [CD track 10 - 16]   10

Lesson 3 – Classic Rock Soloing [CD track 17 - 30]   13

Lesson 4 – Classic Rock Arpeggios [CD track 31 - 44]   16

Lesson 5 – Double Stops [CD track 45 - 54]   19

Lesson 6 – Garage Rock [CD track 55 - 64]   22

Lesson 7 – Developing Speed [CD track 65 - 70]   25

Lesson 8 – Whammy Bar [CD track 71 - 84]   28

Lesson 9 – D Tuning [CD track 85 - 91]   32

Lesson 10 – Two-Handed Tapping [CD track 92 - 98]   36

INTRODUCTION

This book contains ten lessons on rock and metal guitar playing, and has been designed to be used both by tutors and students of the guitar. Tutors will find the book extremely effective as a teaching aid, as it contains ready-made lessons through which pupils can be guided.

Students will find that the lessons are presented in an accessible and informative manner, and that by listening to, and playing along with, the examples on the CD their playing will quickly improve.

HOW TO USE THIS BOOK

Each lesson consists of the main lesson text, followed by several musical examples in both music notation and tablature. The musical examples are all demonstrated on the accompanying CD. The CD track relevant to the example is shown above the notation with this symbol: ⊙ **5** – e.g. track 5 on the CD.

Backing tracks for many of the examples are also included on the CD, so that the reader can play along with a musical accompaniment. The CD track number is given above the examples with backing tracks.

A tuning guide is provided on track 1 of the CD.

REGISTRY OF GUITAR TUTORS

This book was written by Tony Skinner, Director of the Registry Of Guitar Tutors

The Registry Of Guitar Tutors (RGT) is the world's foremost organisation for guitar education. RGT has a membership of thousands of registered guitar tutors, not only in the UK but also in many countries across the world.

GAIN A GUITAR PLAYING QUALIFICATION

RGT compiles examinations in electric, acoustic, bass and classical guitar – from beginner to diploma level. These are organised in partnership with London College of Music Examinations, one of the world's leading music examination boards. The examinations are accredited by the Qualifications and Curriculum Authority (QCA) and, for higher grades, also by the Universities and Colleges Admissions Service (UCAS).

You can study for an RGT exam from home with a course handbook, or via lessons with a local tutor. (Contact the RGT if you need to find a registered guitar tutor in your area.)

Studying for an RGT examination will help you develop your guitar playing in a structured and comprehensive way. To find out which level exam grade your playing is at, view the RGT website www.RegistryOfGuitarTutors.com or call the RGT for a free exam information pack on 01424 222222 (or 0044 1424 222222 from outside the UK).

NOTATION GUIDE

All of the music examples in this book are written in both traditional music notation and tablature (TAB).

MUSIC NOTATION

Music for the guitar is traditionally written using the treble clef. The illustration below shows a range of notes on the treble clef – from the low open E string to the 12th fret on the high E string.

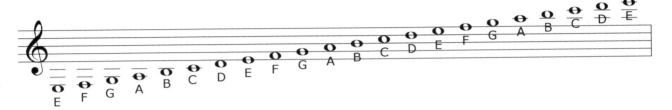

A sharp (♯) before a note would raise its pitch by a semitone (i.e. one fret higher), whilst a flat (♭) before a note would lower its pitch by a semitone (i.e. one fret lower). A natural sign (x) before a note cancels a sharp or flat sign.

TABLATURE

TAB is a system of notating guitar music that uses horizontal lines to represent the strings – with the top line representing the high E (1st) string and the bottom line representing the low E (6th) string.

Numbers on the lines indicate the fret number. A zero on a line indicates that the string should be played open (i.e. unfretted).

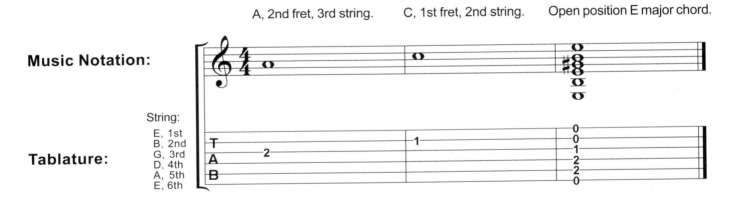

READING RESOURCES

If you need help in reading music notation, a wide range of sight-reading books specifically for guitarists is available at:
www.BooksForGuitar.com

Notation Symbols

String Bend (& Release)

Bend string up (BU) to the pitch of the note in brackets. Let string down (BD) to original note pitch.

Hammer-on & Pull-off

Hammer-on (H): Pick the first note, then sound the higher note by fretting without picking.
Pull-off (P): Pick the first note, then sound the lower note by pulling finger off string.

Slide

Pick the first note, then, whilst keeping pressure on the fingerboard, move down (or up) to the note indicated.

Palm Muting

Dampen the notes by resting the strumming hand lightly on the strings just in front of the bridge.

Arpeggiated Chord

Bring out the individual notes in a chord by strumming across the strings in the direction indicated.

Fret Hand Damping

Use the fretting hand to dampen the strings whilst they are being struck by the strumming hand.

Natural Harmonics

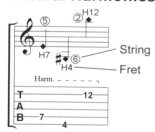

Pick the string indicated whilst lightly resting the finger on the fret at the position shown.

Vibrato

Vary the pitch of the note slightly by making small repeated movements with the fretting hand / finger.

Staccato

The note is played short and detached.

Two-Handed Tapping

Circled notes are sounded by the pick hand striking the string at the fret shown. Notes in squares are sounded by the fret hand tapping the string.

Repeat Directions

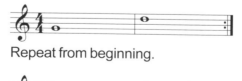

Repeat from beginning.

Repeat music between 'double dot' signs.

Repeat the previous bar.

Other Performance Directions

L.V. Allow strings to ring.

1/4 Quarter Bend – bend note slightly sharp.

POWER CHORDS

PLAYING ONLY SELECTED NOTES FROM A CHORD CAN OFTEN GIVE A STRONGER SOUND THAN PLAYING THE WHOLE CHORD – ESPECIALLY WHEN YOU ADD DISTORTION.

Although open-position chords and barre chords are ideal for some styles of music, you can get a much tighter and more easily controlled sound by just using two or three notes from a chord – especially when using an overdriven sound. In rock music, the most popular types of these smaller, crisper chords are 'fifths' – commonly known as 'power chords'. Apart from the tone, one of the main advantages of using fifths is that it's much easier to change quickly from one chord to another.

To play a fifth power chord, simply fret a note on any bass string and add a note two frets up on the adjacent higher string. In order to play power chords clearly make sure that you adjust your hand stretch to the size of the fret you're playing at: frets get narrower as you move higher up the fretboard. Also, try to move your whole hand when you change fret position – don't try to reach just with the fingers, make sure the thumb of the fretting hand also changes position. Finally, beware of hitting unwanted open strings – only strum the strings that you are actually fretting.

POWER CHORDS IN USE

In the 1970s bands like Black Sabbath and Judas Priest pioneered the use of riffs played in fifths, often adding an octave note to the chord to get an even more powerful sound.

In the 1990s, grunge bands like Nirvana, Pearl Jam and Sound Garden, relied heavily upon the use of fifths in nearly all their songs – although they tended to use a less distorted sound than their metal predecessors. They also often used down and up strokes, rather than the typical rock technique of just muted downstrokes. Many current rock and metal bands base much of their rhythm playing on fifth power chords, often using dropped tunings to create an even stronger sound.

Exercise 1: 5th Chords Based On Different Bass Strings ⊙ 2　　Backing track: ⊙ 3

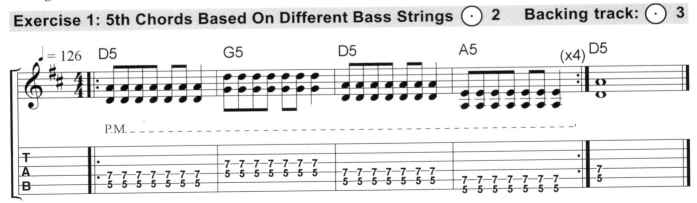

To get a real rock tone, use downstrokes throughout and rest the side of the strumming hand against the strings, near the bridge, to mute the sound.

Exercise 2: 5th Chords In Various Styles   ⊙ 4   **Backing track:** ⊙ 5

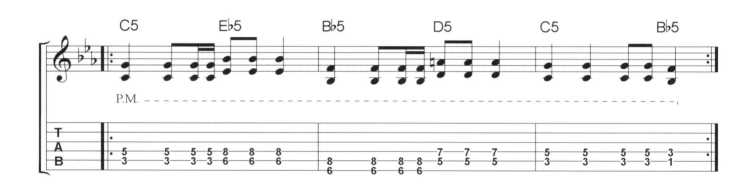

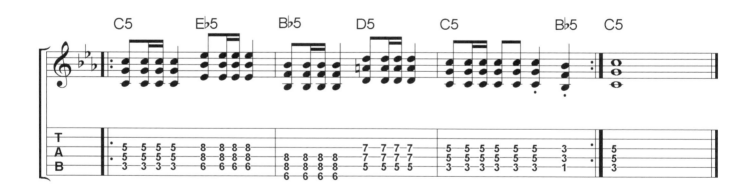

In the first 4 bars the fifth chords are played by picking the notes individually. In the next 4-bar section, the two strings of each fifth chord are played together with a slightly muted sound. In the final 4-bar section, the octave is added and the mute is released to create a very powerful sound.

Exercise 3: Power Chords With The 5th In The Bass   ⊙ 6   Backing track: ⊙ 7

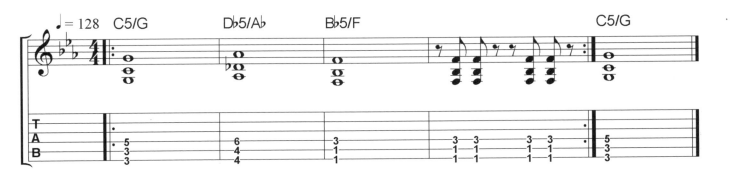

The root note of each chord is on the 5th string, but the fifth note within each chord is 'doubled' by being played on the 6th string (in a lower octave) as well as on the 4th string.

Exercise 4: Power Chords Using Dropped D Tuning   ⊙ 8   Backing track: ⊙ 9

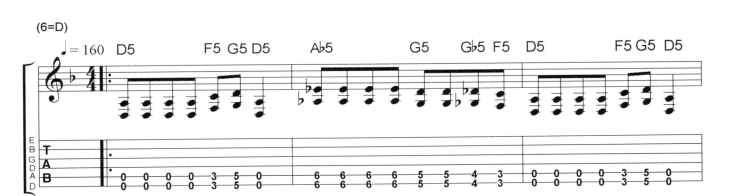

The low E string is de-tuned to D. This enables fifth power chords to be played on the 6th and 5th strings on a single fret – making fast chord changes much easier. This technique is covered in depth in Lesson 9.

CLASSIC ROCK RIFFING

FORGET CHORDS AND LEAD SOLOING, CLASSIC ROCK RIFFS OF THE '60S AND '70S MAKE FOR SOME OF THE MOST MEMORABLE GUITAR PLAYING OF ALL TIME.

Ask any guitarist to list some of their favourite bits of guitar playing and there's no doubt that included in there will be some of the classic rock riffs from the '60s and '70s. Groups like The Kinks and The Rolling Stones in the 1960s, using blues influences, were some of the first rock players to base entire songs around repeated riffs. This approach was further developed in later years by bands like Led Zeppelin, Deep Purple, AC/DC and ZZ Top. Since then, nearly every rock band from Nirvana to Franz Ferdinand has included a riff as the central core of their most popular songs.

RIFFING

A riff is a short melodic phrase that has a strong rhythmic hook. It is usually repeated many times within a song, so that it becomes memorable. Riffs are often played in place of chords, and when this occurs riffs are commonly played on the bass strings in order to give a full and powerful sound. Riffs need not be complex: even just three carefully selected notes played forward and backwards can have real musical impact (exercise 1, CD track 10). Keith Richard's riff in The Rolling Stones' *Satisfaction* is as simple as this, yet it remains one of the most instantly recognisable pieces of guitar playing.

DEVELOPING RIFFS

Extending a riff across more than one octave of a scale can give it a great sense of melodic range, whilst still being quite easy to play (exercise 2, CD track 11). Many classic rock riffs are based on the pentatonic minor scale, but other scales, particularly the blues scale, were used by guitarists such as Jimi Hendrix and Eric Clapton. A blues scale riff is demonstrated in exercise 3 (CD track 12).

DOUBLE STOPS

As riffs are often played instead of chordal rhythm playing, using double-stops (i.e. sounding two notes at once) can help to give depth and strength to the sound of a riff (exercise 4, CD track 13). Jimmy Page of Led Zeppelin often used this technique.

When double stops are used, riffs will sometimes sound powerful enough when played on the treble strings (exercise 5, CD track 14).

Sometimes power chords can be added to single note bass runs to make riffs sound even stronger (exercise 6, CD track 15). Angus Young of AC/DC was a great pioneer of this style of playing. To get a really powerful rock sound, an entire riff can be played completely with power chords (exercise 7, CD track 16).

Exercise 1: E Pentatonic Minor Riff

⊙ 10

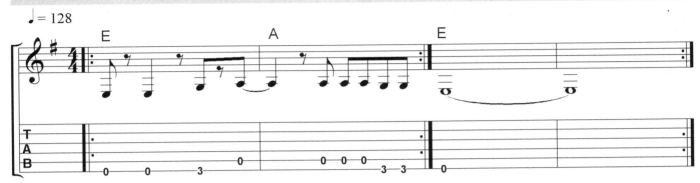

This riff consists of the first three notes of the E pentatonic minor scale. Observe the rests within the music as they form an integral part of the riff.

Exercise 2: E Pentatonic Minor Extended Riff

⊙ 11

This riff extends beyond the one octave E pentatonic minor scale by using the open G string. Notice how bar 2 is a variation of bar 1. The rests at the end are essential to capture the rhythmic character of the riff.

Exercise 3: E Blues Scale Riff

⊙ 12

The use of the ♭5 (B♭) note lends this riff a bluesy flavour.

Exercise 4: Riff With Double-Stop

⊙ 13

The open 6th string is followed by a double stopped 5th and ♭5th diad. Using hammer-ons in the final bar will help with speed and smoothness.

Exercise 5: Double-Stopped Treble Strings Riff

In this riff the 1st and 2nd strings are always played together. Use the 1st finger to fret the notes at the 3rd fret, and the 3rd finger to fret the notes at the 5th fret.

Exercise 6: Riff Including Power Chords

⊙ 15

Care needs to be taken to ensure that the correct number of strings are strummed when playing this riff; getting carried away and hitting extra notes could sound nasty!

Exercise 7: Power Chord Riff

⊙ 16

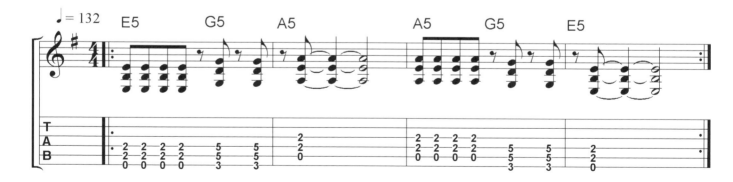

This riff uses the same 3 notes as exercise 1, but this time all the notes are played as power chords. A different rhythmic pattern is also used.

CLASSIC ROCK SOLOING

WHILST NEW STYLES OF PLAYING COME AND GO, THE ROCK SOLOING OF THE '60s, '70s AND '80s IS STILL THE MOST INFLUENTIAL OF ALL LEAD GUITAR STYLES.

The first pioneers of lengthy electric guitar improvisations in a rock music setting were Eric Clapton and Jimi Hendrix in the late 1960s. Clapton had previously played in blues bands, and the increasingly commercial Yardbirds, but by the time Hendrix arrived on the UK rock scene Clapton had formed Cream – a rock trio with improvisation at its heart. Whilst this format freed up his playing style, underpinning it was still an innate reliance on the blues scale and bluesy phrasing (exercise 1, CD tracks 17 & 18). Hendrix at first also still retained very evident blues roots in his playing style (exercise 2, CD tracks 19 & 20).

By the early 1970s, players like Jimmy Page of Led Zeppelin had moved on from a blues style of playing and helped develop a distinctive rock style of guitar – often much more reliant on the pentatonic minor scale than the blues scale (exercise 3, CD tracks 21 & 22).

This new style of playing was in no small part due to the role Hendrix had played, especially in the latter part of his career, in expanding the vision of electric guitar players in how the pentatonic minor scale could be used in rock playing (exercise 4, CD tracks 23 & 24).

OTHER SCALES

In the early 1970s Deep Purple was a band that further developed the musical range of rock music, often by adding classical elements to their sound. Their guitarist Ritchie Blackmore had a particularly melodically inventive and expressive style of lead playing, and often used a variety of minor scales, such as the natural minor, in his soloing (exercise 5, CD tracks 25 & 26).

Of course, rock soloing needn't always be based on minor scales. Paul Kossoff from Free often preferred to use the pentatonic major scale. By combining this with string bending and his passionate vibrato, a powerful bluesy rock sound could be achieved despite the major tonality (exercise 6, CD tracks 27 & 28).

On the other side of the Atlantic, country-rock bands, such as Lynyrd Skynyrd, continued to use the pentatonic major scale as the basis of their playing with great commercial and musical success (exercise 7, CD tracks 29 & 30).

EXAMPLE SOLOS

In this lesson there are seven short classic rock solos in the styles described above. Once you've listened to each one, you'll find a backing track for each is provided for you to play over. Start with the notated solos and then try out your own improvisation over each backing track.

Exercise 1: Blues Scale Solo 1   🎧 17   Backing track: 🎧 18

Notice how the slur in bar 1 includes a hammer-on to the 3rd string, without that string having been picked before. You'll need to hammer hard, with the very tip of your finger, in order for this note to sound clearly.

Exercise 2: Blues Scale Solo 2   🎧 19   Backing track: 🎧 20

Use a strong, but relaxed, slurring action to play the 4-note slurs in bar 3; only the first of each set of 4 notes should be picked with the plectrum hand.

Exercise 3: Pentatonic Minor Solo 1   🎧 21   Backing track: 🎧 22

Bend the last note of this solo with your little finger, but use the other fingers behind it on the same string to add strength and support. Never try and bend a note using only your 4th finger – you could easily injure it!

Exercise 4: Pentatonic Minor Solo 2   🎧 23   Backing track: 🎧 24

As this example is very scalic in approach, warming-up on the A pentatonic minor scale first will provide great preparation for the fast runs.

Exercise 5: Natural Minor Solo

25 Backing track: 26

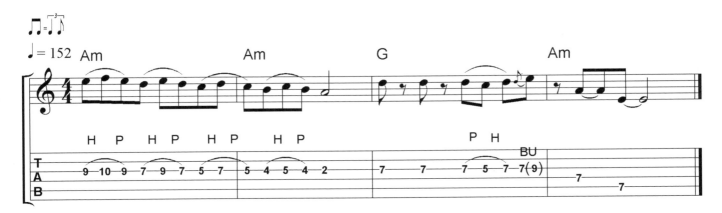

This solo uses slurs from the A natural minor scale descending along the G string. When executed well, this technique creates a smoothness of tone. The backing track has been made double length so that, for comparison, you can try the solo without slurs.

Exercise 6: Pentatonic Major Solo 1

27 Backing track: 28

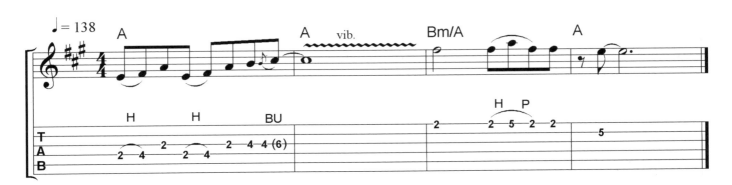

This example uses the A pentatonic major scale. It features some slurs and a bend followed with vibrato.

Exercise 7: Pentatonic Major Solo 2

29 Backing track: 30

Using the lower range of the A pentatonic major scale towards the end lends a slight country rock flavour to this example.

CLASSIC ROCK ARPEGGIOS

ARPEGGIOS AREN'T JUST TECHNICAL EXERCISES; THEY'RE GREAT FOR SOLOING AND CAN MAKE YOUR LEAD PLAYING MORE MELODIC.

An arpeggio is simply the notes of a chord played individually. For example, if you look closely at the open position E minor chord you'll notice that although you're playing six strings there are in fact only three different notes (E G B) in the chord. If you play these notes consecutively, rather than strum them simultaneously, this forms the E minor arpeggio. Each basic major or minor arpeggio will only contain three notes; you can work out which notes these are by analysing the relevant chord shape.

Another method is to take the 1st, 3rd and 5th notes of the major scale with the same starting note (for example, D, F# and A are the 1st, 3rd and 5th notes of the D major scale and so form the D major arpeggio). To work out minor arpeggios flatten the 3rd note of the major arpeggio by a semitone (e.g. D minor arpeggio contains D, F and A).

USING ARPEGGIOS

When you use a scale for a lead solo you'll have noticed that some notes sound less resolved against certain chords than other notes. This problem disappears when you use arpeggios: because the notes of each arpeggio are taken from the chord they will all sound completely 'in tune' – providing you're playing the right arpeggio for each chord. If you've only used scales before, this takes a little getting used to, as you'll need to change arpeggio every time there is a chord change.

PRACTISING ARPEGGIOS

When you're first learning arpeggios it's helpful to practise them in the set order (1st, 3rd, 5th); once you know them you can mix the order up and improvise freely. If you haven't used arpeggios for soloing before, start by beginning each arpeggio lick on the root note (exercise 1, CD tracks 31 & 32).

Once you feel confident with this approach you can use other chord tones as your starting point for each arpeggio (exercises 2, 3 & 4, CD tracks 33 - 38).

ARPEGGIOS IN USE

Most players feel that a solo made up entirely of arpeggios can be almost too 'in-tune', so once you've practised your arpeggio playing it's best to incorporate elements of it with standard scale based lead playing (exercises 5 & 6, CD tracks 39 - 42).

Just listen to almost any solo by classic rock guitarists such as Mark Knopfler, Jimmy Page, Joe Walsh or Paul Weller, and you'll hear this combination of scale and arpeggio playing.

You can also incorporate string bends into your arpeggio playing (exercise 7, CD tracks 43 & 44).

Exercise 1: Rock Arpeggio 1

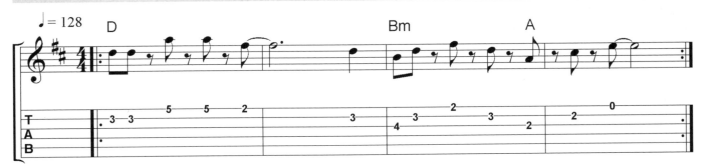

This example uses arpeggios for D major (D F# A), B minor (B D F#) and A major (A C# E); each one starting with the root note of the accompanying chord.

Exercise 2: Rock Arpeggio 2

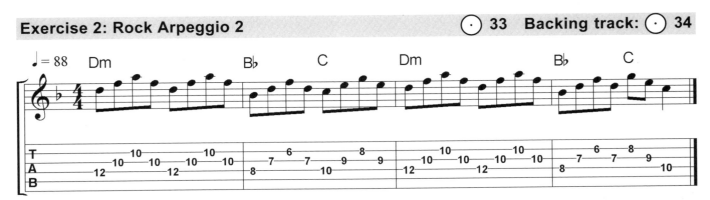

This example begins by using the root note as the starting point for each arpeggio, until the final bar when the highest of the 3 notes is used to start each lick.

Exercise 3: Rock Arpeggio 3

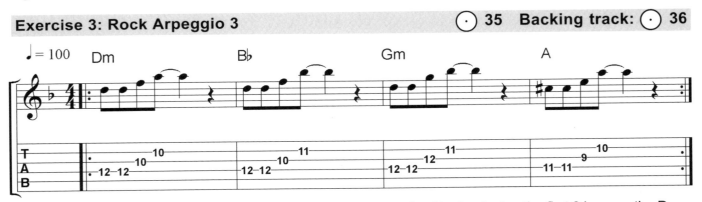

In this example, the similarities between each chord are emphasised by beginning the first 3 bars on the D note, as this note occurs in all 3 arpeggios.

Exercise 4: Rock Arpeggio 4

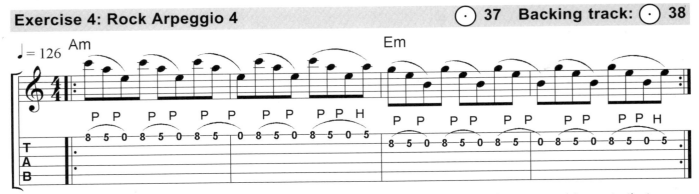

A slurred pattern is played for each arpeggio. This example takes advantage of the open string note that occurs in each chord. Notice how the minor 3rd of each chord is used to start each pull-off.

Exercise 5: Rock Arpeggio 5

39   Backing track: 40

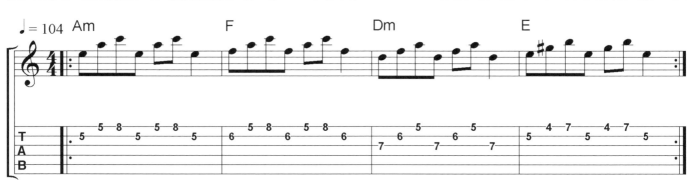

This is a good example of the effective use of chord tones in arpeggio playing: if you were just using the A pentatonic minor scale to solo over this chord progression, you'd lose some of the melodic finesse that can be achieved with arpeggios (such as the use of the G♯ note over the E major chord).

Exercise 6: Rock Arpeggio 6

41   Backing track: 42

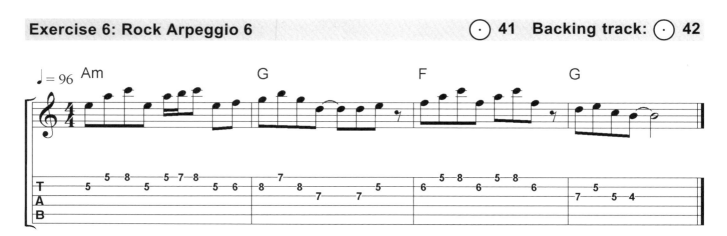

Whilst this solo is still very strongly arpeggio based, it goes beyond the range of notes that occur solely in the arpeggios and also includes passing notes from the A natural minor scale.

Exercise 7: Rock Arpeggio 7

43   Backing track: 44

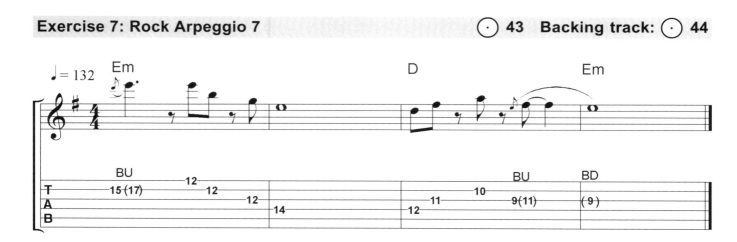

String bends can be used with arpeggios in exactly the same way as with other styles of lead playing.

DOUBLE STOPS

ONCE YOU HAVE EXPERIENCED THE SOUND OF TWO NOTE (DOUBLE-STOP) PLAYING YOU'LL NEVER WANT TO PLAY A SINGLE NOTE LEAD SOLO AGAIN!

Double-stopping is the technique of playing two notes at once. Early blues players pioneered this technique, but it was Chuck Berry in the 1950s, using an electric guitar, who really brought the technique into widespread popularity. Since then his double-stop licks have been emulated by many guitarists – as diverse as Jimi Hendrix, Steve Jones and Angus Young.

BEGIN DOUBLE STOPPING

The best way to begin double-stopping is to experiment with fretting two notes at once in a pentatonic minor scale; laying your fretting-fingers flat across two strings on the same fret. In order to make both notes sound at once, when playing them on the same fret, you'll need to lay your fingers slightly flat against the fretboard and press with the pads rather than the tips of your fingers. The sound of double-stopping is so strong when compared to single-note playing that you'll find you can get a great sound without having to rush around the fretboard too much.

Double-stops can be played from any scale. In theory you can combine any two notes from a scale, but some combinations will sound better resolved than others, depending upon the backing chords. You should feel free to experiment with any pairs of notes within a scale: it's only by trying different double-stops that you'll discover which ones you like the sound of. However, if you want to play safe, you can start by choosing any two notes that are separated by only one note within the scale (e.g. A and C♯ from the A major scale). This approach will normally result in an interval of a 3rd or 4th (depending upon the scale used): such an interval will normally work quite well over most chords, and is therefore a fairly reliable starting point.

In this lesson five examples of classic double-stop riffs have been notated in a range of musical styles. Once you have learnt these, have a go at making up some of your own.

Exercise 1: Static Double-Stops   🔘 **45**   **Backing track:** 🔘 **46**

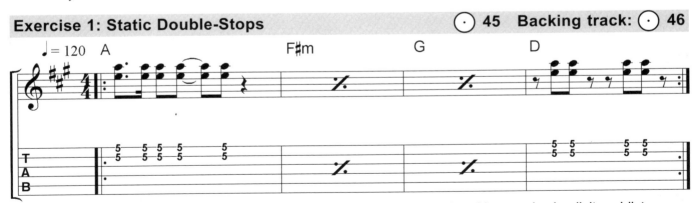

The power of double-stops enables you to use melodic understatement and harmonic simplicity, whilst creating an effective rhythmic groove. U2's The Edge often uses double-stop playing in this way. Use an echo unit to emulate the U2 sound.

Exercise 2: Double-Stop Riff With Slides ⊙ **47   Backing track:** ⊙ **48**

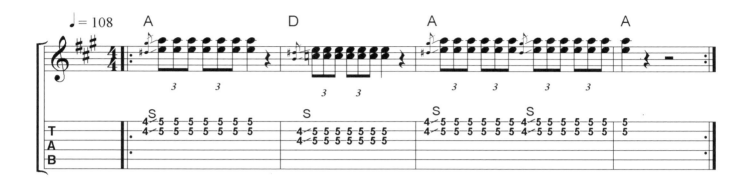

Sliding into each of these double-stopped riffs from a fret below will help give a feeling of energy and momentum to the performance.

Exercise 3: Single Position Double-Stop Riff ⊙ **49   Backing track:** ⊙ **50**

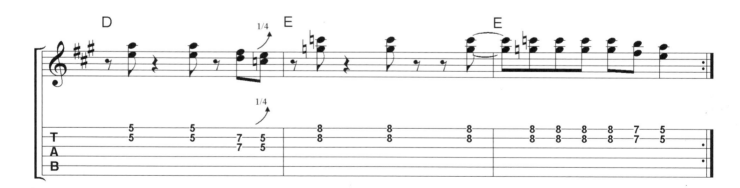

This Chuck Berry style riff demonstrates how you can stay on a one-position riff whilst the other band members do the work of changing chords. Chuck normally used a semi-acoustic Gibson ES355 or 350T. If you're using a solid body guitar you can get emulate the sound by increasing the mid and low range frequencies on your amp, and adding just a touch of reverb and mild distortion.

Exercise 4: Double-Stops In A Minor Key   · 51   Backing track: · 52

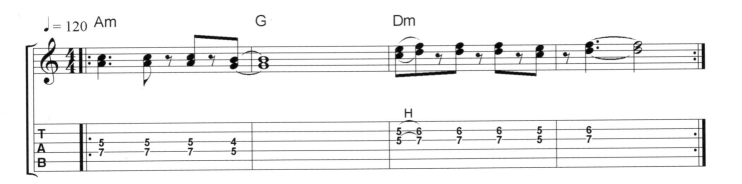

These double-stops are all taken from the A natural minor scale. Guitarists as wide ranging as Buddy Guy, Jimi Hendrix and Mark Knopfler have often used this scale in this way.

Exercise 5: Double-Stops In A Major Key   · 53   Backing track: · 54

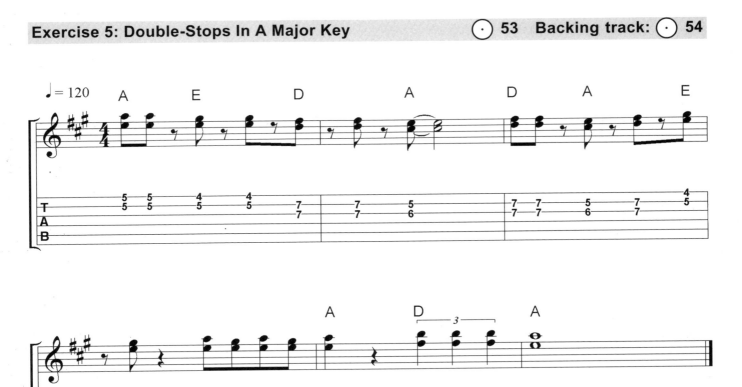

These double-stops are all taken from the A major scale. Using double-stops in a major key is a useful way of boosting the inherently delicate sound of the major scale.

GARAGE ROCK

LEARN HOW TO PLAY RIFFS AND LEAD LINES USED BY GARAGE ROCK GROUPS SUCH AS THE WHITE STRIPS, THE VINES, THE STROKES AND THE DATSUNS.

The term 'garage rock' first originated in the USA in the 1960s with young bands rehearsing fairly raw rock music in their parents' garages. Most of the techniques used by the later crop of garage rock bands hark back to the no-frills approach used by seminal sixties rock bands such as the MC5s and, in the UK, the Kinks. The low-fi recording techniques emulated by many contemporary garage rock bands give the records a classic feel. The influence of punk bands, such as The Ramones, and the raw power of metal bands, like Motorhead, is also evident.

DAMPING

There are several techniques commonly used by the newer breed of garage rock bands, the most popular being chord damping whilst playing a straight eighth-note pattern. This is achieved by placing the palm of the picking hand on the strings and playing downstrokes to create a staccato effect. This technique also facilitates the use of accents by varying the strength of the damping (exercise 1, CD tracks 55 & 56). This muted sound is often contrasted by using heavily distorted chords without damping; the playing style is much more open using both down and upstrokes to create more volume and sustain (exercise 2, CD tracks 57 & 58).

OTHER GARAGE TECHNIQUES

When recording, to create a much bigger sound, bands like The Strokes often use 'multi-tracking' (recording the same guitar part more than once). A technique regularly used by several garage bands such as The Strokes and The Vines is to play chords on the off-beat using upstrokes (a style taken from Ska music). This is a tricky technique that must be combined with muting with both the palm of the picking hand and by lifting-off the notes on the fretting hand to create notes of the desired length - being careful not to let any notes ring out in the gaps (exercise 3, CD tracks 59 & 60).

Many garage rock riffs involve using 5th power chords with a punchy, staccato rhythm, in a typical Kinks style (exercise 4, CD tracks 61 & 62).

LEAD LINES

Garage bands tend to use fairly simple but very effective lead techniques. For example, a lead line typical of a band like The Strokes would involve a very heavily distorted guitar sound and a simple line often played on just two strings. Slides are often used, so that the lead is played in a linear fashion up the fingerboard instead of on adjacent strings (exercise 5, CD tracks 63 & 64).

Exercise 1: Palm Muted Chord Riff ⊙ 55   Backing track: ⊙ 56

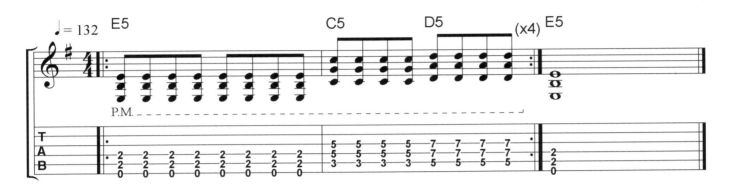

Play all the chords with downstrokes, keeping the rhythm as tight as possible. Practise controlling and varying where you place the accents.

Exercise 2: Heavy Chord Riff ⊙ 57   Backing track: ⊙ 58

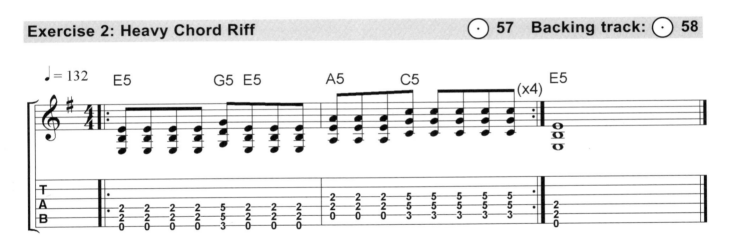

Use a heavily distorted sound with the classic 5th power chord shape to create a typical garage rock riff.

Exercise 3: Upstroke Offbeat Riff ⊙ 59   Backing track: ⊙ 60

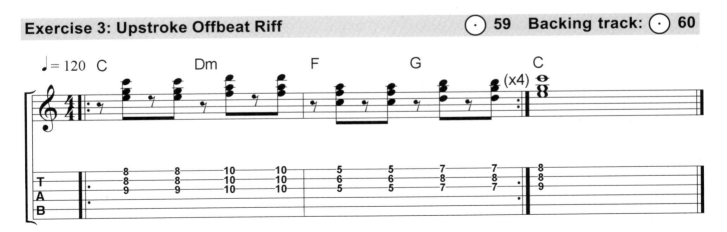

Strike only the top three strings, using upstrokes. Use damping and muting to control the length and power of each chord.

Exercise 4: Punchy Chord Riff

61   **Backing track:** 62

Make sure that you observe the rests after each chord – this gives a strong punchy sound that would be absent if all the chords were allowed to ring-on. Open string vamps may help the changes between chords.

Exercise 5: Lead Line

63   **Backing track:** 64

Using a highly distorted sound and playing across just a couple of strings with techniques like sliding you can create typical garage rock lead licks.

DEVELOPING SPEED

AS WELL AS IMPROVING YOUR TECHNIQUE SO THAT YOU CAN PLAY MORE FLUENTLY, THERE ARE OTHER WAYS YOU CAN MAKE YOUR PLAYING 'SOUND' FASTER.

Nearly all electric guitarists want to play fast – it's something that seems to be in the blood! However, fast playing relies upon using the plectrum in the optimum way – hold the plectrum the wrong way and you can slow down your playing for years to come. The best method is to grip the plectrum between the thumb and index finger. Position the plectrum so that its point is 'just' beyond the fingertip: if you show too much plectrum it will drag against the string; too little and you may miss the string altogether. Be careful not to use too much pressure when gripping the plectrum, as this will make your hand muscles tighten and so reduce your fluency. To gain speed, it's essential that you repeatedly alternate down and up plectrum strokes: to simply pick in one direction is akin to trying to sprint whilst hopping on one leg! If you've never used alternate picking before, it may feel more difficult at first, but in the long run this technique will allow you to achieve much greater speed and fluency. Once you have a good plectrum technique you can make your licks sound faster by doubling, or even quadrupling, your picking on some notes. The fretting hand may be moving quite slowly, but the lick will sound more mobile because of the activity of the picking hand. Practise this technique at first by playing scales with double and quadruple picking (exercises 1 & 2, CD tracks 65 & 66).

USING SLURS

'Slurring' comprises two main techniques: 'hammering-on' and 'pulling-off'. Each of these techniques allows you to sound two or more notes for each pick of a string - enabling you to play both smoother and faster. To 'hammer-on' a note, don't pick the string again – instead, rapidly and firmly hammer the tip of your finger right next to the fretwire of the note that you want. The note should come out almost as clearly as if you had picked it normally. If you're doing it right the string should leave an imprint on your fingertip! (exercise 3, CD track 67). To 'pull-off' a note, first fret a note, then pull your fretting finger lightly downwards until it plucks the string, and the lower fretted note is sounded. Avoid just 'lifting' your finger off into the air – you have to make a slight 'downward' movement for the note to sound clearly. Practise this technique at first by playing a pentatonic minor scale – hammering the notes on the way up and using pull-offs on the way down .

TRIPLETS

A great way of making your playing sound fast is to use 'triplet patterns' - playing three notes in the time of one beat, and repeating some notes of the scale within these patterns. Because these patterns cut across the standard 4/4 rhythm, they deceive the listener by giving the impression of being much faster than they really are. The example given uses the A pentatonic minor scale (exercise 4, CD track 68).

Once you've got your fingers round all these techniques try playing along with the demo track, (exercise 5, CD track 69). A backing track is also provided for you to make up your own solo (CD track 70).

Exercise 1: A Pentatonic Minor Scale Double Pick (slow, then fast) 65

A pentatonic minor scale – double picked. Make sure that you alternate down and up plectrum strokes.

Exercise 2: A Pentatonic Minor Scale Quadruple Pick (slow, then fast) 66

A pentatonic minor scale – quadruple picked. Try not to grip the plectrum too tightly – the more relaxed your hand is, the easier this picking becomes.

Exercise 3: A Pentatonic Minor Scale Hammered-On (slow, then fast) 67

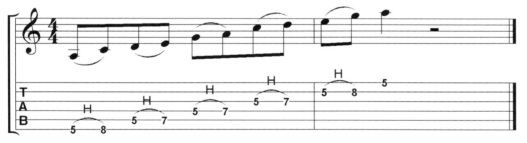

A pentatonic minor scale – hammered-on. Hammer close to the fretwire using the tip of your finger.

Exercise 4: A Pentatonic Minor Scale Ascending In Triplets (slow, then fast) 68

A pentatonic minor scale – ascending in triplets. This triplet pattern consists of playing a note of the scale, then the note below in the scale, and then back to the original note. Play this same pattern starting from each note of the scale.

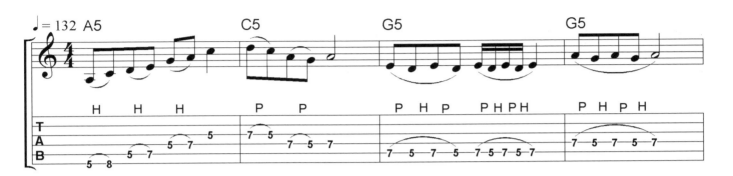

This track involves all the techniques mentioned in this lesson: use it to practise these skills. Slurs can be used on the triplets if preferred.

WHAMMY BAR

THE WHAMMY BAR CAN BE ONE OF THE MOST EXPRESSIVE TOOLS AVAILABLE TO THE ELECTRIC GUITARIST – THIS LESSON SHOWS YOU HOW TO GET THE MOST OUT OF IT.

The great thing about the whammy bar is that it can is used in such a wide variety of ways – from the very subtle to the downright extreme. Consequently, no matter what style of music you might be playing, the whammy bar can often add that extra something to give your playing a lift.

PIONEER

Hank Marvin of The Shadows was one of the first British guitarists to pioneer the use of the whammy bar (then known as the tremolo arm), and to this day he remains one of the true experts of the technique – often called "the master of the melody" because of his ability to use the bar to make his guitar lines expressive and almost vocal-like.

WHAMMY TECHNIQUES

The whammy bar can be used simply as a way of adding vibrato (either subtle or wide) to a note, by gently but repeatedly raising the bar up and down (exercise 1, CD tracks 71 & 72). In fact, this was what the bar was first invented for. This technique generally works best on notes either at the start or end of a phrase, or on any individual notes that you might wish to emphasise – but, just as with a vocal performance, too much vibrato can sound contrived; so use this technique with care and thought.

CHANGING PITCH

By pushing or pulling the bar a little further you can actually change the pitch of the note – rather like bending a string. You can lower a note by pushing the bar inwards (exercise 2, CD tracks 73 & 74), or you can raise a note by pulling the bar upwards (exercise 3, CD tracks 75 & 76). It takes some practice, but you'll soon begin to get a feel for the amount of pressure needed in order to reach the exact pitch of the note you require; notice that less whammy bar movement is required to alter the pitch of notes higher up the fingerboard compared to lower fretted notes.

SPECIAL EFFECTS

The whammy bar need not be restricted to single notes – it also works really well with chords: giving a keyboard-like effect to a single strummed chord (exercise 4, CD tracks 77 & 78). Rock players from Ritchie Blackmore and Jeff Beck to Van Halen and Steve Vai have extended the range of whammy bar techniques with effects like 'dive bomb' (depressing the bar to lower the note fully until the strings are completely slack – exercise 5, CD tracks 79 & 80) and combined the use of the whammy bar with harmonics to create some startling sounds (exercises 6 & 7, CD tracks 81-84).

Exercise 1: Whammy Vibrato

Shake the whammy bar up and down very slightly to get this typical Shadows style vibrato.

Exercise 2: Downward Dip

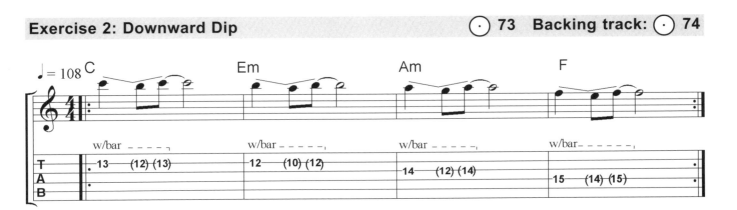

Depress the whammy bar to achieve these downwards dips in pitch, and then release the bar back to return each note to its original pitch. Note the different amount of pressure that is required between the semitone and whole tone shifts.

Exercise 3: Upward Rise

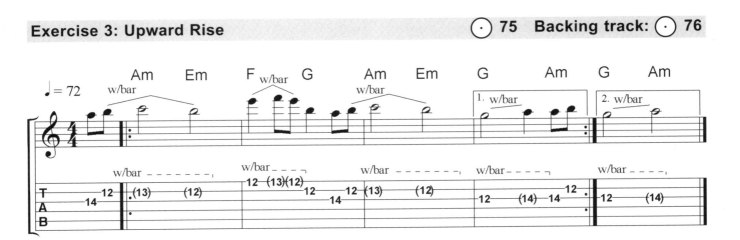

Pull the whammy bar upwards to raise the notes, releasing the pressure when you wish to come back down in pitch.

Exercise 4: Chord Vibrato

⊙ 77   Backing track: ⊙ 78

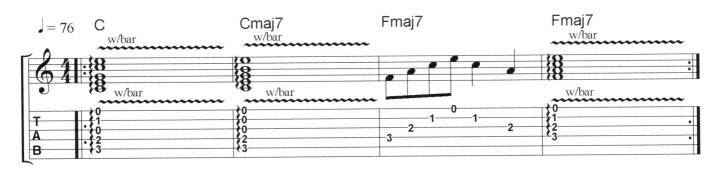

When striking a single chord, a quite strong but steady movement of the whammy bar will result in a powerful sweeping sound.

Exercise 5: Dive Bombing

⊙ 79   Backing track: ⊙ 80

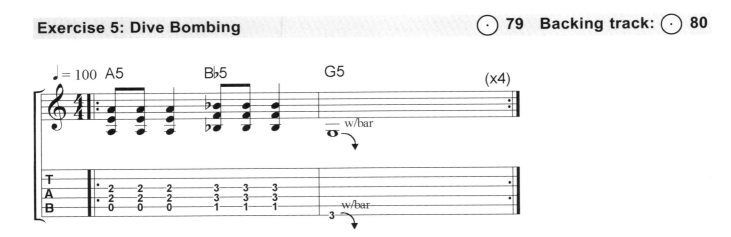

In this example, the whammy bar is gradually fully depressed to create a 'dive bombing' effect.

Exercise 6: Combining Harmonics

⊙ 81   Backing track: ⊙ 82

The A and E notes are only picked once but the whammy bar is then firmly flicked inwards with the picking hand palm 6 times to give the repeat short gargle effect. The natural harmonic notes at the 7ᵗʰ fret are bent down and released back up with the whammy bar.

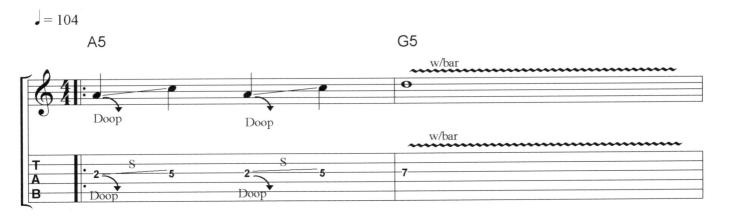

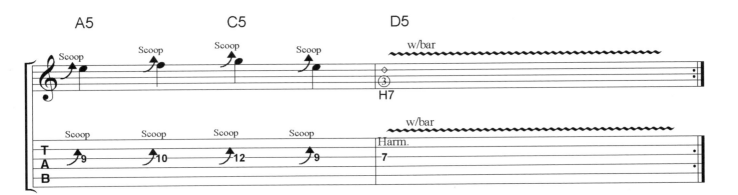

The first lick uses a doop down (lowering the whammy bar just after the picking the note) followed by a fretboard slide. Bar 3 begins with some scoops (lowering the whammy bar slightly before each note is played and then releasing). The phrase ends with a rapid harmonic vibrato.

D TUNING

GET DOWN AND DIRTY BY DETUNING YOUR LOW E STRING TO D; THE SOUND CAN BE EXTREMELY POWERFUL.

Dropping the pitch of the low E string down to D is a great way of extending the range of your guitar. The sound can become very dark and powerful, which is why metal players often favour this technique. If you're trying this for the first time, you can judge when the sixth string becomes tuned to D by playing at the 12th fret as you lower the pitch: this should give the same note as the open fourth (D) string.

Once the string has been detuned remember that all the fretted notes on that string will sound a whole-tone lower than before. For example, the note on the third fret of the sixth string will now be F, rather than G as it would be in standard tuning. Although this means that your normal six-string chord shapes will no longer work, it does open up a whole host of other playing possibilities.

PLAYING LOW

The most obvious advantage of D-tuning is that you can reach a lower note than you could with standard tuning. The low D note will have a lot of depth and resonance that is unattainable in standard tuning. Playing a riff, or ending a phrase, on the low D note is a good way to begin getting familiar with the new tuning (exercise 1, CD track 85).

In order to make the most of its tonal character, you can even play complete riffs just on the low D string (exercise 2, CD track 86).

POWER CHORDS

One of the reasons D-tuning is used so much in metal and rock is that you can play 'power chords' (the core of metal and rock rhythm playing) with only one finger in this tuning (exercise 3 & 4, CD tracks 87 & 88). The low D string is also great for creating a 'drone effect': the open sixth string is strummed repeatedly whilst notes or chord shapes are moved about on the higher strings (exercise 5, CD track 89). Similarly you can use the sixth string as a 'pedal tone' by playing a series of chords but always coming back to strike the open sixth string between each chord change (exercise 6, CD track 90).

ARPEGGIOS

Of course, you don't always need to use strumming: playing chords and picking the strings, with the fingers or plectrum, when using D-tuning can give a very deep and melancholic sound (exercise 7, CD track 91).

Exercise 1: D-Tuning Riff Across 3 Strings

⊙ 85

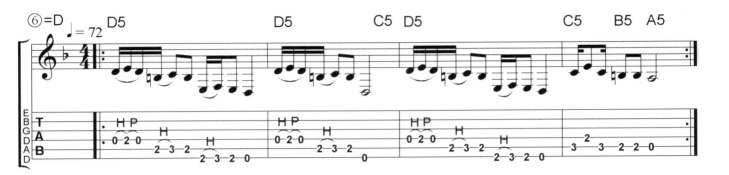

Notice the use of slurs to create a smooth flowing sound. If you're reading the treble clef notation remember that low E will now be found on the 2nd fret of the 6th string.

Exercise 2: D-Tuning 6th String Riff

⊙ 86

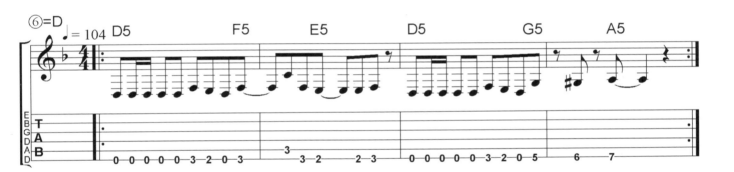

Apart from the C note, all of this riff can be played on the 6th string.

Exercise 3: D-Tuning Strummed Power Chords

⊙ 87

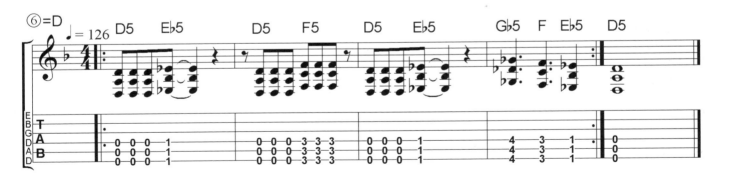

All the power chords in this example can be played solely with the first finger across the bottom three strings. Be careful not to strike the treble strings.

Exercise 4: D-Tuning Strummed And Picked Power Chords

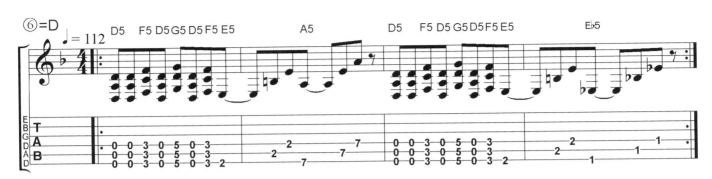

Although this whole progression could be played solely with the first finger, to save moving around, you might prefer to use the third finger on the G5 chord.

Exercise 5: D-Tuning Drone Progression

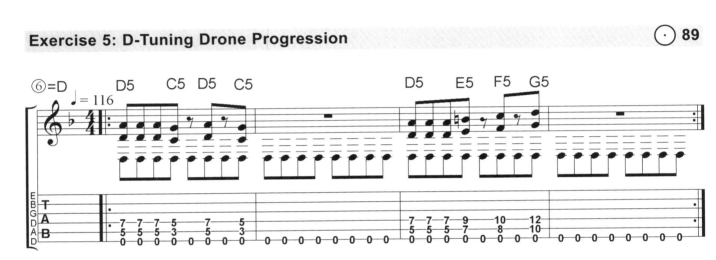

Make sure that you keep strumming the open 6th string throughout this progression, and only strum the other bass strings when a chord occurs.

Exercise 6: D-Tuning Chords And Pedal Tone

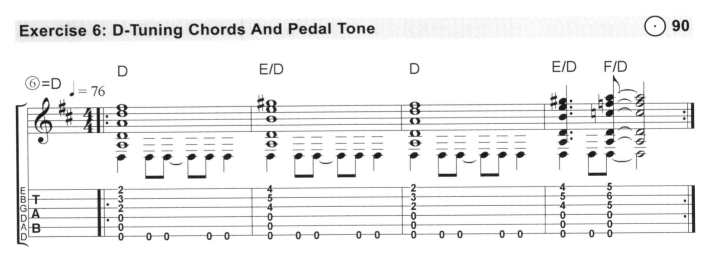

This typical '70s rock progression is based on an open D major chord shape moved up and down the fingerboard, whilst using the open low D as a pedal tone.

Let all the notes of the chord ring-on throughout each bar. Notice how the picking pattern (6123 123 6545) remains the same for each chord, except for a small variation in the final bar.

TWO-HANDED TAPPING

INSTEAD OF JUST USING ONE HAND TO FRET AND SLUR NOTES, INSTANTLY DOUBLE YOUR POTENTIAL BY USING BOTH HANDS.

Rather than using a plectrum to pick a note, you can produce a similar sound purely by tapping the string firmly against the fretboard using a finger from either the left or right hand. If you've never tried tapping before then it's easiest to start with pick (right) hand one-finger tapping. If you're playing a whole solo of tapping you could jettison the pick and use your first finger to tap, however many players prefer to keep the pick ready between the first finger and thumb and use the second finger to tap notes. Whichever finger you use, make sure that you tap with the bony tip of the finger, rather than the soft fleshy pad, in order to get the clearest sound. You can angle your tapping finger so that it is inline with the fretboard (horizontal tapping) or position the tapping finger at right angles to the fretboard (vertical tapping) – either method will suffice for basic tapping patterns, but vertical tapping technique will provide you with more possibilities as your playing develops.

TAPS AND SLURS

Tapping is often combined with pull-offs to create fast legato runs (exercise 1, CD track 92). Eddie Van Halen was one of the first players to fully exploit this style of playing. After a tap you can pull-off to a note by moving your finger in either a downward or upward direction. Players such as Randy Rhoads and Nuno Bettencourt often play arpeggio or scale figures, with the high tapped notes being taken from the same scale or arpeggio as the fretted notes (exercises 2 & 3, CD tracks 93 & 94).

Guitarists such as Joe Satriani and Steve Vai sometimes incorporate open strings into the tap/slur combinations, as this makes fast patterns easier to play (exercises 4 & 5, CD tracks 95 & 96). Tapping notes with the fret (left) hand (i.e. hammering-on to fret a note without previously picking that string) expands the range of melodic and harmonic possibilities. For example, you could combine different fingerboard positions within a chord: playing some notes low with fret hand taps and some high up the fretboard using pick hand taps (exercise 6, CD track 97). If you're feeling adventurous you could even using each hand to tap two or more notes simultaneously (exercise 7, CD track 98). Stanley Jordan is one of the masters of this style of two-handed tapping.

TAPPING TIPS:

- The lower the action on your guitar the easier it is to produce notes clearly when tapping.
- Make sure that your guitar's intonation is set-up accurately, as the large interval leaps that tapping allows will highlight any intonation problems.
- Many tap specialists use a string damper near the nut in order to minimise the unwanted ringing of adjacent strings.
- Tapping is easiest on an electric guitar with powerful pick-ups; try adjusting your pick-ups so that they are close to the strings.
- Using compression will help disguise any volume imbalances between notes.

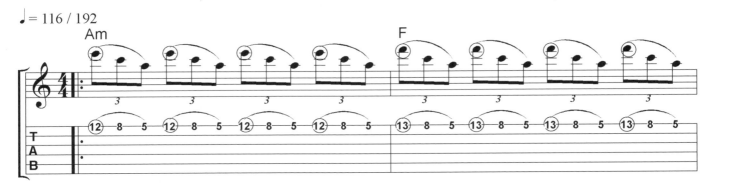

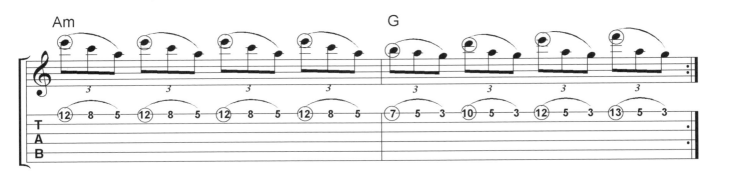

This example consists of three-note patterns that each begin with a pick hand tapped note; this is then pulled-off to a fretted note, which in turn is pulled-off to another fretted note. The tapped notes are circled. For simplicity and clarity, all the usual slur symbols (P & H) have been omitted on the notation.

Exercise 2: Pick Hand Tapping With Scale Licks – Slow & Fast   ⊙ 93

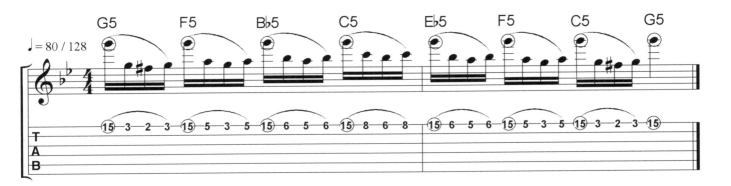

The pick hand tapped note is always the high G; the fretted notes are taken from the G harmonic minor scale played along the first string. The tapped notes are circled. For simplicity and clarity, all the usual slur symbols (P & H) have been omitted on the notation.

Exercise 3: A Pentatonic Minor Scale With Tapping – Slow & Fast   ⊙94

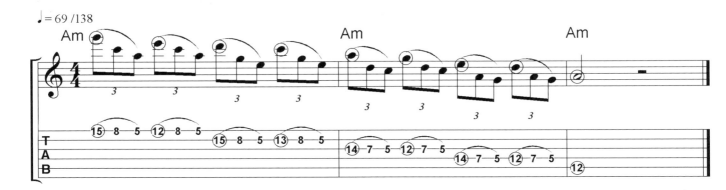

The A pentatonic minor scale is fretted in 5th position, and combined with a tapped version of the scale in 12th position. All the tapped notes are circled. Each is followed by two pull-offs.

Exercise 4: Two-Handed Octave Tapping – Slow & Fast   ⊙ 95

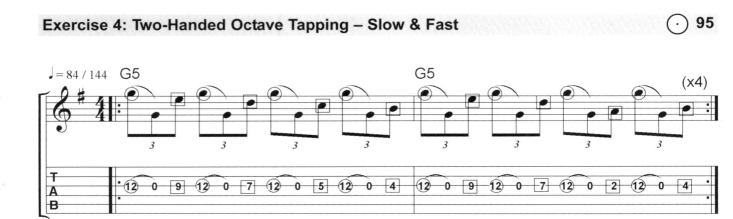

The pick hand taps the high G note, which is then pulled off to the open G string. This is followed by fret hand taps along the G string, playing notes from the G major scale. Fret hand tapped notes are marked in squares.

Exercise 5: Tapping And Slurring To Open Strings – Slow & Fast   ⊙ 96

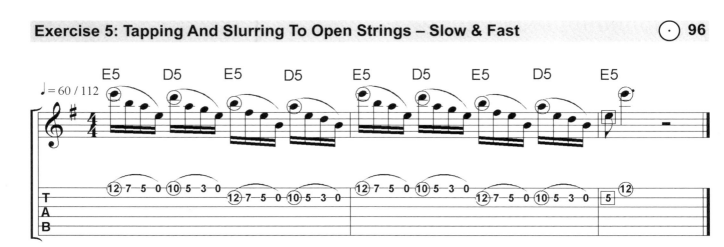

In this lick both the tapped note and the fretted patterns shift along the fretboard; each four-note phrase ends with an open string. Pick hand taps are circled. The fret hand tap is shown in a square.

Exercise 6: Two-Handed Tapped Arpeggios – Slow & Fast

◷ 97

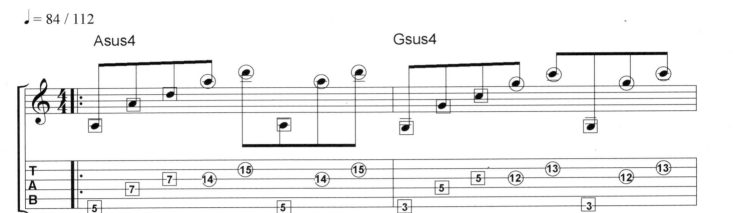

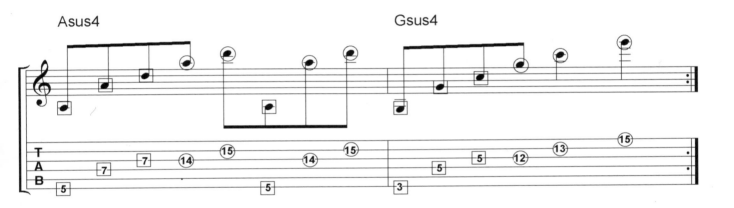

To get a legato sound, tap the fret hand notes rather than pick them. No notes are picked in this example; everything is tapped with either the left or right hand. This is an advanced technique and will require plenty of practice.

Exercise 7: Double-Stopped Tapping – Slow & Fast

◷ 98

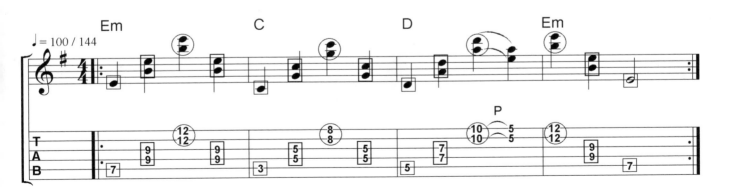

This example features two-finger tapping with both left and right hands – no notes are picked. Aim to get the volume of all notes fairly even. This may be difficult at first, but as the saying goes: "Practice makes perfect".